LYDIA

and the present

Shoo Rayner

Oxford University Press

Oxford University Press, Walton Street, Oxford OX2 6DP

Oxford   New York
Athens   Auckland   Bangkok   Bombay
Calcutta   Cape Town   Dar es Salaam   Delhi
Florence   Hong Kong   Istanbul   Karachi
Kuala Lumpur   Madras   Madrid   Melbourne
Mexico City   Nairobi   Paris   Singapore
Taipei   Tokyo   Toronto

and associated companies in
Berlin   Ibadan

Oxford is a trade mark of Oxford University Press

First published 1987
Reprinted 1987, 1989, 1991, 1994, 1995
Printed in Hong Kong

ISBN 0 19 916174 7

The Lydia books are:

Lydia and her garden
Lydia and the letters
Lydia and the present
Lydia and her cat
Lydia at the shops
Lydia and the ducks

Lydia book pack: ISBN 0 19 916171 2

It was Lydia's birthday.
'Hooray!' said Lydia.

She got dressed.

There was a huge parcel for her.

'What is it?' asked Lydia.

'You can make things with it,' said Mum.

They made a boat to play in.

Lydia pretended to be a lion at the zoo.

They made a table.

They made a house.

Lydia learned to walk on stilts.

'I'm very tired,' said Lydia.

'I know what we can make,' said Mum.

What a useful present!